GYMNASTICS

Gymnastics Competitions

ON YOUR WAY TO VICTORY

by Jen Jones

Consultant
Connie Dickson
Minnesota State Chair
USA Gymnastics Women's Program

Capstone
press

Mankato, Minnesota

Snap Books are published by Capstone Press,
151 Good Counsel Drive, P.O. Box 669, Mankato, Minnesota 56002.
www.capstonepress.com

Library of Congress Cataloging-in-Publication Data
Jones, Jen, 1976–
    Gymnastics competitions : on your way to victory / by Jen Jones.
    p. cm. — (Snap books. Gymnastics)
    Summary: "A guide for children and pre-teens on competitive
gymnastics scoring and skills needed to excel in competitive gymnastics"—
Provided by publisher.
    Includes bibliographical references and index.
    ISBN-13: 978-0-7368-6467-1 (hardcover)
    ISBN-10: 0-7368-6467-9 (hardcover)
    1. Gymnastics—Competitions—Juvenile literature. I. Title. II. Series.
GV461.3.J34 2007
796.33—dc22   2006005999

Editor: Wendy Dieker
Designer: Jennifer Bergstrom
Illustrator: Renée Doyle
Photo Researcher/Photo Editor: Kelly Garvin

Photo Credits: AP/Wide World Photos/Amy Sancetta, 26–27; Capstone Press/Karon Dubke, cover, 8–9; Corbis/
NewSport/Rick Rickman, 17 (right); Corbis/Reuters/Kimimasa Mayama, 29; Corbis/Reuters/Reinhard Krause, 24–25;
Corbis/S. Carmona, 7 (rhythmic gymnast); Getty Images Inc./AFP/Robyn Beck, 23; Getty Images Inc./Bongarts/
Christof Koepsel, 7 (acrobatic gymnasts); Getty Images Inc./Sean Garnsworthy, 17 (left); Getty Images Inc./Stephen
Dunn, 12–13; Getty Images Inc./Stuart Hannagan, 4–5; Jennifer Jones, 32; SportsChrome Inc./Empics, 3 (top), 14–15;
SportsChrome Inc./Michael Zito, 3 (middle, bottom), 6 (artistic gymnast), 11, 19, 20–21; SportsChrome Inc./Sport the
Library, 7 (trampoline gymnast)

1 2 3 4 5 6 11 10 09 08 07 06

TABLE OF CONTENTS

14-15

18-19

20-21

Features

Visions of Medals

'Twas the night of the Olympics, and all through the land, little girls dreamed of medals in their hands.

When the Olympics are shown on television, women's gymnastics is often the event with the most viewers. Millions tune in. They want to watch the gymnasts twist and tumble. Little girls watch medalists like Carly Patterson take the gold. They often dream about winning the same honor. The good news is that competitive gymnastics is open to anyone. You just need to have the desire to succeed!

Though only a few reach the Olympics, thousands of other competitions take place every year. Many gymnasts get a chance to show their stuff. In this book, you'll learn about the different types of competitions. You'll also learn about what the judges look for in each gymnastics event. Competition isn't easy. Yet the rewards make the hard work worth it.

Carly Patterson

Gymnastics 101

Gymnastics is likely to hold something that fits your fancy!

THE WIDE WORLD OF GYMNASTICS

This book centers mainly on artistic gymnastics, the traditional **program**. But did you know that many different programs exist in competitive gymnastics?

Just for girls, rhythmic gymnastics displays graceful movements set to music. Gymnasts tumble and dance while holding props like hoops, ribbons, and balls.

Artistic

Trampoline

Acrobatic

Rhythmic

The feats in trampoline gymnastics use the bounciness of the trampoline. Women reach heights of up to 30 feet (9 meters) in the air!

In acrobatic gymnastics (or "acro"), gymnasts work in teams to show their balance and strength. They build amazing pyramids and towers with their bodies.

Acting Local, Going Global

After making the decision to compete, the next step is to join a gymnastics club. It's best to find one that is a member of USA Gymnastics. USA Gymnastics is a group that oversees many local, regional, and national competitions. It is also the group that oversees selection of the U.S. National Team. Being part of a member gym gives you a VIP pass to move up in the ranks!

The International Gymnastics Federation (FIG) has the same role as USA Gymnastics on a global level. It is the job of the FIG to make rules for each gymnastics program. Another must-know organization is the U.S. Olympic Committee. This group supports and trains Olympic team members for the big event!

Rising Through the Ranks

No matter the age, gender, or skill level, there is a competition for everyone. Once a gymnast turns 6 years old, she becomes eligible for USA Gymnastics competitions. These competitions pave the road to the Olympics. Beginners start at Level One. To rise through the skill levels, gymnasts must pass tests given by their coaches. Gymnasts in Levels One through Nine usually compete at local and regional competitions, or "meets."

The most advanced gymnasts reach Level Ten. These competitors go on to big national championships. After reaching Level Ten, a gymnast becomes "Elite." She can then set her sights on Olympic gold.

Yet even at small, local meets, the crowning moment is the awards ceremony. The top-scoring gymnasts receive medals and recognition. Wouldn't you look great with a medal around your neck?

BY THE NUMBERS

In 2004, more than 62,000 women took part in competitions **sanctioned** by USA Gymnastics. Of those gymnasts, only 1,900 were at Level Ten and 143 were considered Elite.

Inside the Action

During a gymnastics meet, there is rarely a dull moment! Picture the scene: up to four gymnasts performing at the same time on a sprawling floor with a section for each **apparatus**. Music is playing for the floor exercise while another girl is vaulting. An amazing **dismount** from the bars is happening while a gymnast on the beam does a cat leap. Judging panels for each event are stationed around the floor. Audiences must divide their attention among their favorite gymnasts or events. So much is happening at once, it's impossible to see it all!

On a Pedestal

Events usually take place on a raised stage so that the judges can see the gymnasts from the sidelines more easily.

Gymnasts usually have three chances to earn a medal.

In **All-Around** competition, a gymnast competes in all four events. Her scores from each event are added together to determine an overall winner.

Individual medals are given for the best performances on each of the four apparatus.

In **Team** competition, several gymnasts from each team compete in the four events for a combined score.

Sometimes, the scores from one performance count for all three competitions. At other meets, gymnasts perform once for each chance at a medal.

Judging and Scoring

Get out your calculators! It's all about math when scoring a competition.

The perfect 10 is now a thing of the past! In 2006, the International Gymnastics Federation introduced a new code of points for international competitions. Under the new code, two panels of judges score the performance. The "A" panel is made up of two judges who monitor difficulty. The "B" panel of two to four judges keeps tabs on how well the gymnasts perform.

9 8 5

On the "A" panel's watch, the gymnast works upward from a zero score by adding as many difficult elements as possible. From the "B" panel, the gymnast starts with a score of 10. The panel then subtracts points if technical and artistic performances are sloppy. To come up with a gymnast's final score, the "A" and "B" scores are added together. It's a numbers game with some serious stakes!

Easy as ABC

Gymnastics moves are ranked with letters. In Elite competition, an easy move is ranked A, while the toughest moves are ranked with a G. G-level moves get the most points.

The Keys to the Vault

In the vault event, a gymnast takes flight in hopes of earning her wings—in medal form! A vault routine is lightning-quick. It consists of four parts: the run, pre-flight, post-flight, and landing. Depending on the competition, gymnasts are allowed one or two vaults. If she gets two, the average of the scores is the final score.

Achieving top speed during the run gives strength to the vault. During pre-flight (the launch from springboard to vault table), judges keep an eye out for proper body positioning. For post-flight (the mid-air moment between pushing off and landing), gymnasts are scored on the height, distance, and difficulty. Finally, judges look at the landing. Did she "stick" it perfectly? All of these factors play into the final score.

Vault Musts

* both feet must jump off the springboard for pre-flight
* pre-flight must be in forward or backward position—no side entries
* both hands must push off from the table for post-flight
* landing must be within marked lines on mat

Buzzworthy Beam Routines

In routines that last up to 90 seconds, gymnasts must cover all 16 feet (5 meters) of the balance beam. They perform acrobatic moves that are challenging on the ground, let alone up in the air! The key word? Balance. Without it, a gymnast may fall to the ground. Each fall is a **deduction**. Confidence and concentration are needed to keep the routine flowing smoothly. The judges make deductions if a gymnast pauses before a difficult move.

A gymnast may be required to perform a series of two or more connecting elements. For example, she could do a back handspring into a back somersault. Also required are turns, leaps, and a difficult dismount. Each of these elements counts toward the final score. It's important that they are not missing from the mix!

Beam Musts

* routine must cover the length of the beam
* 180-degree leap, jump, or hop is required
* must include a forward or sideward acrobatic element
* routine must include a backward acrobatic element
* dismount required

Unbelievable on the Uneven Bars

"Go with the flow" just might be the unofficial motto of the uneven bars event. After all, gymnasts are scored on how well they flow from one move to the next without pausing. Moves such as handstands and twists are required during a routine. Plus, there must be a great dismount. Twists or flips in the dismount will gain points.

Along with a good flow, release moves are also required. A gymnast must let go of a bar and catch another to show her release moves. Strength, instinct, and power are needed to impress the judges. The slightest timing mistake or weak grip can cause the gymnast to fall to the ground. Landing on the mat before the dismount is a deduction from the final score.

Bar Musts

* must show release moves: high bar to low, low bar to high, and on the same bar
* include giant circles
* close-bar elements, such as hip circles required
* dismount required

23

Fabulous Floor Exercise Routines

Show tunes and classical music. Dazzling acrobatics, dancing, and tumbling. These elements make up the floor exercise routines. In the space of 90 seconds, gymnasts must cover the entire mat area. They do many tumbling runs designed to wow the crowd. Dance moves such as leaps, turns, and leg stretches fill the space between tumbling passes.

Flexibility, elegance, energy, and personality take the front lines in scoring. Gymnasts who lose steam after doing several tumbling passes will lose points. Stepping out of bounds also results in subtracted points. In this event, judges are looking for creative self-expression through movement and personality. Body control and a mastery of tumbling are key.

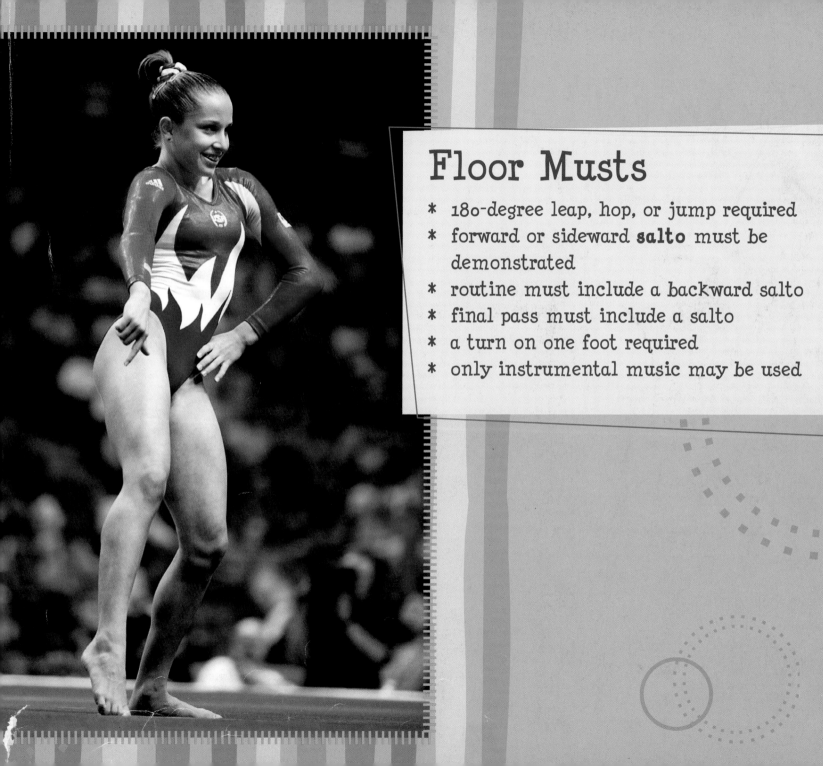

Floor Musts

* 180-degree leap, hop, or jump required
* forward or sideward **salto** must be demonstrated
* routine must include a backward salto
* final pass must include a salto
* a turn on one foot required
* only instrumental music may be used

③ Competition Secrets

The secrets of making it to the top are revealed!

Training Time

Just like models don't wake up with their hair perfectly in place and a camera-ready face, gymnasts aren't made overnight. The journey from Level One to Elite gymnast takes years. And it takes a high degree of dedication. Training for competition can feel like a full-time job. Some gymnasts spend as many as 50 hours in the gym every week. Besides regular practice, gymnasts must also make an effort to eat well and keep fit with other kinds of exercise.

To master seemingly impossible gymnastics skills, gymnasts need to be mentally prepared as well. Gymnasts picture themselves doing a skill perfectly. The hope is that the mental game will equal victory in real life!

"You have to be mentally strong and prepared to take on the workload of going to the gym every day, rain or shine."

–Shannon Miller, U.S. Olympic medalist

25

Fearless Leaders

Training for the big time is no easy task. Having a good coach by your side is the best way to win the gold. Gymnastics coaches act as leaders and teachers. They sometimes even act as second families. Spending long hours training in the gym often gives gymnasts and their coaches a close bond. However, coaches don't always play nice. Some coaches are tough on their team members. They push their girls to make it to the top. Legendary Olympic coach Bela Karolyi is one example of this approach. He churned out Olympic champions like Nadia Comaneci, Mary Lou Retton, and Dominique Moceanu.

Big Time Coach

For 30 years, Bela Karolyi was a coach in Romania and the United States. His successful trainees include 28 Olympians, nine Olympic champions, 15 World champions, 12 European medalists, and six U.S. National champions.

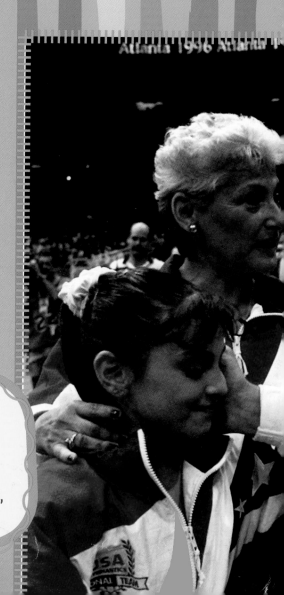

Bela Karolyi

When gymnasts "graduate" from the competitive world, many go on to become coaches. It's a great way to stay involved with what they love and what they do best. For example, former Olympic champions Nadia Comaneci and Bart Conner are now married. They run a gym together in Oklahoma. Olympic medalist Dominique Moceanu coaches up-and-comers in Ohio.

You've Got the Look

You never get a second chance to make a first impression! Many gymnasts take that old cliché to heart when appearing before the judges. After all, no one wants to lose points for looking messy or unsure. Girls pull their hair back in a neat ponytail or bun and wear very little makeup.

Leotards are the outfit of choice. The stretchy fitted fabric is lightweight and moves easily. In Team competition, the members of the team all wear matching leotards. As far as fancy footwork, gymnasts go barefoot for most events. Tumbling shoes are sometimes worn for floor exercise or beam routines.

Most important is projecting an air of confidence. And now that you know what competitive gymnastics is all about, that should be easy. Remember, if you don't believe you can do it, no one else will!

"All the careful assessment of the opposition in the world can't substitute for self-confidence and tip-top physical condition."

—Nadia Comaneci, Romanian Olympic medalist

Glossary

apparatus (ap-uh-RAT-uhss)—equipment used in gymnastics, such as the balance beam or uneven bars

deduction (dee-DUK-shuhn)—subtraction of points from the score

dismount (DISS-mount)—a move done to get off of an apparatus

program (PROH-gram)—a type of gymnastics; some programs include artistic, rhythmic, and acrobatic.

salto (SAHL-toh)—a flip with the feet coming over the head and the body rotating around the axis of the waist

sanction (SANGK-shuhn)—to give permission to compete under an organization's name and rules; USA Gymnastics sanctions gyms to hold USA Gymnastics tournaments.

Fast Facts

Youngest Youngster
At age 14, Dominique Moceanu became the youngest U.S. gymnast to win an Olympic gold medal. She helped the U.S. team take the gold in 1996.

Never Too Old
Though many gymnasts retire in their late teens or early 20s, some keep going into their 30s. Case in point: Cheri Knight-Hunter, a seven-time All-American, competed in her 30s!

Old School
Gymnastics is no newbie to the Olympics. Alongside eight other sports like tennis, swimming, and cycling, gymnastics made its debut in 1896 at the very first modern Olympic Games in Athens, Greece.

Read More

Ditchfield, Christin. *Gymnastics*. A True Book. New York: Children's Press, 2000.

Herran, Joe, and Ron Thomas. *Gymnastics*. Action Sports. Philadelphia: Chelsea House, 2004.

Hughes, Morgan. *Gymnastics*. Junior Sports. Vero Beach, Fla.: Rourke, 2005.

Morley, Christine. *The Best Book of Gymnastics*. New York: Kingfisher, 2003.

Wesley, Ann. *Competitive Gymnastics for Girls*. Sports Girl. New York: Rosen, 2001.

Internet Sites

FactHound offers a safe, fun way to find Internet sites related to this book. All of the sites on FactHound have been researched by our staff.

Here's how:

1. Visit *www.facthound.com*

2. Choose your grade level.

3. Type in this book ID **0736864679** for age-appropriate sites. You may also browse subjects by clicking on letters, or by clicking on pictures and words.

4. Click on the **Fetch It** button.

Facthound will fetch the best sites for you!

About the Author

Jen Jones has been very involved in the cheerleading and gymnastics worlds since she was old enough to turn a cartwheel. Jen has several years of gymnastics training and spent seven years as a cheerleader. After college, Jen cheered and choreographed for the Chicago Lawmen semi-professional football dance team. Today Jen lives in Los Angeles and writes for publications like *Pilates Style*, *American Cheerleader*, and *Dance Spirit*. She also teaches cheerleading, dance, and Pilates classes and is a certified BalleCore instructor.

Index

Washington, D.C.

OUR NATION'S CAPITAL

from A–Z

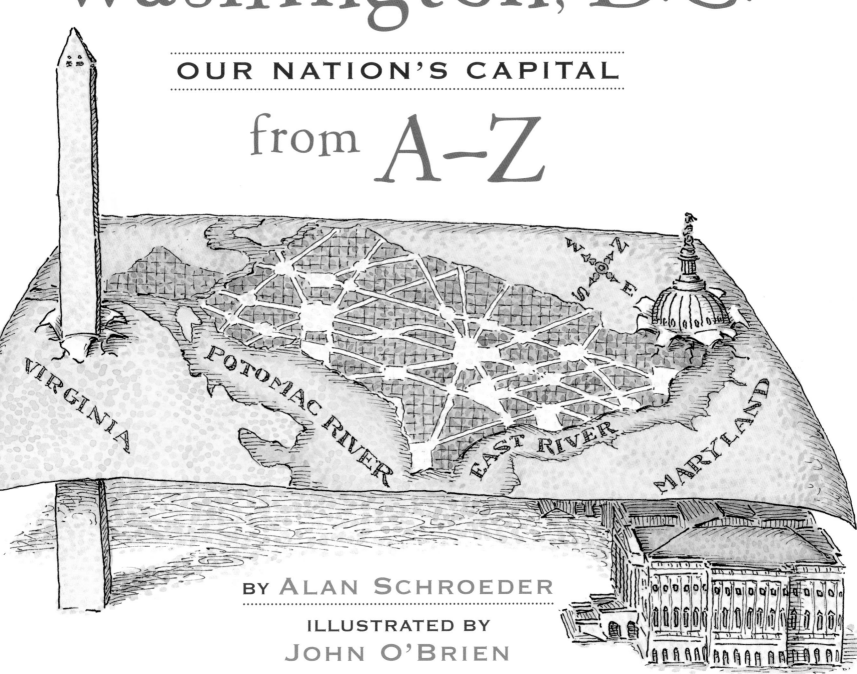

VIRGINIA

POTOMAC RIVER

EAST RIVER

MARYLAND

BY ALAN SCHROEDER

ILLUSTRATED BY
JOHN O'BRIEN

HOLIDAY HOUSE ● NEW YORK

A is for Act

In 1789, when George Washington became president, the nation's capital was New York City—but not for long. A year later, Congress passed the Residence Act of 1790, which changed everything. According to the act, the American government would soon move to Philadelphia, Pennsylvania, where it would remain for ten years. Then, in 1800, the government would move permanently to a spot on the Potomac River in Maryland. It was left up to George Washington to decide the exact location. To no one's surprise, he chose a quiet spot near his home at Mount Vernon.

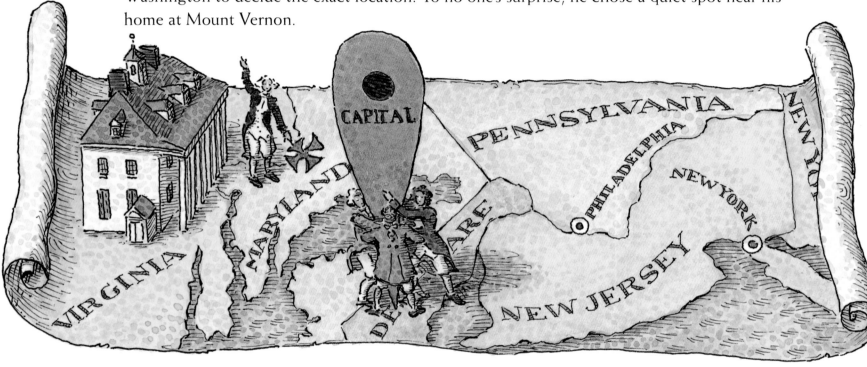

Air and Space—The Smithsonian National Air and Space Museum is one of the city's most popular attractions. If you want to get a close-up look at airplanes, rockets, spaceships, space suits, or ballistic missiles, Air and Space is the place to go!

Acrobat—In 1949, an acrobat named Glenn Sundby walked down the 897 steps of the Washington Monument on his hands. It took him an hour and twenty-five minutes.

"Washington is a city of Southern efficiency and Northern charm."
PRESIDENT JOHN F. KENNEDY

B is for Bull Run

The Battle of Bull Run was the first major engagement of the Civil War. Because the battlefield lay close to the nation's capital, many Washingtonians drove out to watch the fighting; some brought picnic lunches. They assumed that the Union Army would be victorious. To their shock, the Confederates won the battle, and terrified Washingtonians were sent fleeing on foot, on horseback, and in carriages.

Banneker—Benjamin Banneker, a self-taught African American, was one of the surveyors who, in 1791, helped determine the boundaries of Washington, D.C. With the aid of a telescope, he charted the position of the stars to help him lay out the original boundary stones. Banneker was an amazing man. He published a yearly almanac, and built what is believed to be the first clock in America. It kept perfect time for forty years!

Baseball—There used to be a large baseball diamond on the south grounds of the White House. It was called, appropriately, the White Lot. President Andrew Johnson and his staff often went outside to watch the games. President Ulysses S. Grant did more than just watch—he umpired.

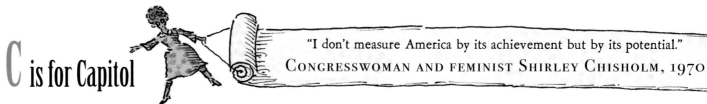

C is for Capitol

The U.S. Capitol is home to the legislative branch of the American government. Here, the Senate and the House of Representatives meet to make the laws that Americans live by. The Capitol opened for business in November of 1800, but construction work on the building continued for another quarter century, until 1826. During those years, the Capitol was a dusty and noisy place to work. Not many people know it, but six large marble bathtubs were installed in the basement of the Capitol in 1860. Congressmen bathed there before and after debates. Any lady who toured the Capitol in those days and took a wrong turn got an eyeful!

The cast-iron dome atop the U.S. Capitol weighs nearly nine million pounds!

Cherry—There are few prettier sights than that of Washington's cherry trees when they are in bloom. The trees, which were planted in 1912, were a gift to our country from Japan. Washingtonians love their cherry blossoms dearly. When the Jefferson Memorial was being built, some trees had to be removed. Washington women chained themselves to the tree trunks in a desperate effort to stop the demolition.

Compromise—Washington, D.C., is in the South, not the North, because of a political compromise. In 1790, Southerners agreed to support a financial plan for the nation that they did not entirely trust. In return, Northerners agreed to place the U.S. capital in the South, and not in New York City or Philadelphia.

Cathedral—Over three hundred feet tall, Washington's National Cathedral is the second-largest cathedral in the United States. Construction began in 1907 and was not finished until 1990. Woodrow Wilson, the nation's twenty-eighth president, is buried here. So are Helen Keller and her teacher, Anne Sullivan.

Cemetery—One of the most solemn sites in the Washington area is Arlington National Cemetery. Here lie the bodies of thousands of American soldiers, statesmen, and prominent citizens. Perhaps the most unusual "resident" is James Parks, a former slave who died in 1929. Parks was actually born at the cemetery; after gaining his freedom, he worked as a gravedigger at Arlington for many years.

D is for District of Columbia

At one time, the city of Washington stood within a larger district that was owned by the federal government. But Washington kept growing, and today the city and the district are geographically the same. The capital was named Washington to honor our first president (George didn't mind). And the district around it was called Columbia in a poetic reference to Christopher Columbus, the man who, the Founding Fathers believed, discovered America. Our nation's capital can be referred to in three different ways: Washington; Washington, D.C.; and the District of Columbia.

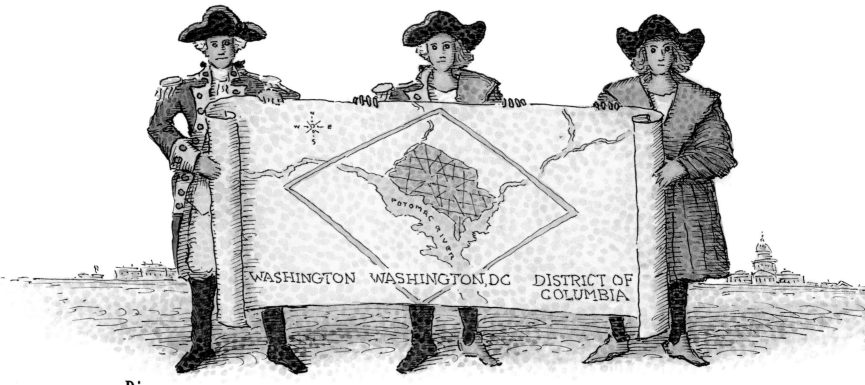

WASHINGTON   WASHINGTON, DC   DISTRICT OF COLUMBIA

Divorce—For many years, no one could quite figure out if Washington, D.C., was its own city or if it belonged to the government. This resulted in some very strange laws. To get a divorce in Washington, for example, required an Act of Congress!

Dinosaur—Millions of years ago, dinosaurs used to roam up and down the East Coast. So many fossils have been found between Washington, D.C., and Baltimore, Maryland, that the area has been called Dinosaur Alley. A large Astrodon thighbone was found beneath the streets of Washington in 1942. Of course, some people would say that dinosaurs still roam Washington. They live in Congress.

E is for Emancipation Day

For many years, a joyous occasion in Washington was the annual Emancipation Day Parade, held on April 16, the day in 1862 when slavery came to an end in the nation's capital. Black Washingtonians celebrated the day with dancing, singing, and a lengthy parade. To this day, the Parade remains a fun family event in Washington, D.C.

Einstein—Most memorials in Washington are meant to be admired from afar. Not the Albert Einstein Memorial on Constitution Avenue. People clamber all over the statue of the brainy physicist. It's said that if you rub Einstein's nose, you get smarter.

"If A is success in life, then A = x + y + z. Work is x, play is y and z is keeping your mouth shut." ALBERT EINSTEIN, 1929

Embassy—Nearly 180 foreign embassies are located in Washington, D.C. Only one city—Brussels, Belgium—has more.

F is for Fire

George Washington believed that placing the U.S. capital on the Potomac would keep the city safe from enemy invasion. During the War of 1812, he was proved wrong. In August of 1814, British soldiers and sailors stormed the capital, whose inhabitants had fled. Still smarting from their defeat in the Revolutionary War, the British took pleasure in setting fire to the Capitol, the White House, and other federal buildings. It took many years, and a vast sum of money, to rebuild the nation's capital.

Freedmen—During and after the Civil War, thousands of black Southerners fled to Washington, D.C. There they found safety but lacked everything else: food, clean water, clothing, shelter, employment, health care, and education. The Freedmen's Bureau, a government organization, tried to help, but fully a third of D.C.'s freedmen died within a few years.

Flag—Though it's not widely known, the District of Columbia has its own flag. It consists of three red stars, two red horizontal bars, and a white background. A 2004 poll named it the best-designed city flag in America.

"I believe that truth is the glue that holds government together, not only our government but civilization itself."
PRESIDENT GERALD FORD, 1974

G is for Grand Review

The FBI has its headquarters in Washington, D.C., on Pennsylvania Avenue.

The Grand Review is remembered as one of the largest celebrations in Washington's history. In May of 1865, shortly after the end of the Civil War, the Army of the Potomac paraded up Pennsylvania Avenue. Thousands lined the sidewalks and stood on rooftops. Nearly 150,000 Union men took part in the Grand Review, which lasted two days. The parade ended not with soldiers, but with a huge herd of cattle, war prizes taken from Confederate farms.

Georgetown

—Founded in 1751, Georgetown is one of Washington's best-known and most attractive neighborhoods. It started out as a port town and is now a favorite destination of tourists, who love to walk and ride alongside its pretty canal. Thomas Jefferson and Francis Scott Key used to live in Georgetown; years later, so did Senator John F. Kennedy. In fact, Kennedy proposed to his wife, Jackie, in a Georgetown tavern.

Gargoyles and Grotesques

—The exterior of Washington's National Cathedral is decorated with numerous gargoyles and grotesques. Some are frightening, some are humorous, some are unexpected. Among the recognizable figures: Darth Vader from the Star Wars films.

Gargoyles are waterspouts, or drains—grotesques aren't.
Darth Vader is a grotesque.

H is for Hunger March

During the Great Depression, hungry people marched en masse to Washington to beg the government for food, work, and other forms of relief. Children stood outside the White House gates on Thanksgiving Day 1932 and sang a heartbreaking song: "Empty is the cupboard, no pillow for the head, we are the hungry children who cry for milk and bread." Instead of being given food, the hungry children were arrested.

Huddle—Football's first huddle took place at Washington's Gallaudet University, the nation's top school for deaf and hearing-impaired students. To share strategies, the deaf athletes formed a huddle, or tight circle, which kept their next play a secret from the other team. Huddles caught on and are now used by all football players.

Hospital—During the Civil War, nearly every government building and church in Washington was turned into a makeshift hospital. Among those who nursed the wounded soldiers was thirty-year-old Louisa May Alcott, who later wrote the book *Little Women*. At first, hospital work frightened her, but she soon found the strength she needed to carry on. "This was no time for nonsense," she said later.

The American Red Cross was founded in Washington, D.C., in 1881.

I is for Indian Museum

A popular Washington, D.C., attraction is the Smithsonian's National Museum of the American Indian, which contains one of the world's largest collections of Indian artifacts. The museum's Mitsitam Cafe is popular with visitors because it serves a variety of Native American dishes, including fry bread, corn totopos—even buffalo burgers!

Illiterate—Before the Civil War, most Washingtonians were illiterate—they could not read or write. To remedy that problem, the city set up a number of public schools. The charge was fifty cents per month. But that was too expensive for most people, and they stayed away. Only when Washington's schools became free did attendance pick up.

Igloo—During a big snowstorm in 2010, a senator and his family built an igloo near the Capitol to poke fun at the idea of global warming.

I-495 is the main highway that surrounds Washington, D.C. Locally, it's known as the Beltway.

J is for Jefferson Memorial

Built during World War II, the Jefferson Memorial is one of Washington's best-known and most elegant structures. Because of wartime restrictions on metal, the statue of Thomas Jefferson inside the memorial had to be made of plaster. Not until after the war ended was the statue replaced with the bronze version that we see today.

The Jefferson Memorial was modeled after the Pantheon in Rome.

Johnson

In 1963, when she became First Lady, Claudia "Lady Bird" Johnson did everything she could to help beautify Washington, D.C., which had become something of an eyesore. She cleaned up the city's playgrounds, planted trees and flowers, painted school buildings, and had unsightly billboards taken down. In her own words, Lady Bird Johnson made Washington "more livable and more beautiful."

J Street

When Washington was laid out, its streets followed the alphabet, A through W. Except for J. There is no J Street. It was felt that the letters "I" and "J" looked too much alike when written out by hand, so to avoid confusion, the letter "J" was dropped.

K is for King

One of the largest gatherings in Washington's history took place on August 28, 1963. On that day, speaking to a crowd of 250,000 people, civil rights leader Martin Luther King, Jr., delivered a memorable speech. "I have a dream," he said, "[that one day my children] will not be judged by the color of their skin, but by the content of their character." Eighty million people, including President John F. Kennedy, watched the rally on television.

Knickerbocker—The Knickerbocker snowstorm has been called the worst blizzard in Washington's history. On January 27 and 28, 1922, a record twenty-eight inches of snow fell, causing many deaths and collapsing the roof of the Knickerbocker, Washington's newest and largest movie theater. Nearly one hundred people lost their lives when the roof caved in.

Kitchen—The kitchens in the White House are underground. Years ago, whenever it rained heavily, the kitchens would flood. Elaborate White House meals were prepared by cooks standing in ankle-deep water.

In 1874, King David Kalakaua of the Hawaiian Islands became the first ruling monarch to visit Washington, D.C.

L is for Library of Congress

The Library of Congress in Washington, D.C., contains one of the world's largest collections of books, manuscripts, music, and photographs. Almost everything is here: nature books, mysteries, a huge collection of cookbooks (including the first cookbook ever published, in 1475), history books, books on spiritualism and magic (donated by Harry Houdini), opera librettos, five million maps, three million sound recordings, and a copy of the Gutenberg Bible. It has been said that if you read one volume every day, it would take 60,000 years to read all the books in the Library of Congress.

L'Enfant—The architect whom George Washington chose to design and build the nation's capital was a Frenchman named Pierre Charles L'Enfant. L'Enfant had grand ideas for the federal city: wide, handsome boulevards, fountains, statues, public gardens, and great buildings made of marble. Unfortunately, L'Enfant cared nothing about budgets. Worse, he was an arrogant man who would listen to no one: he had to have his way all the time. In the end, Washington had to fire him. But much of L'Enfant's plan can still be seen in the city's overall design.

Lobby—In the early 1800s, before Washington, D.C., had any courthouses, trials were held in the lobbies of large hotels on Pennsylvania Avenue. Elections, too.

Lincoln Memorial—Dedicated in 1922, the Lincoln Memorial is one of Washington's most beloved sites. Because it honors Abraham Lincoln, the "Great Emancipator," the Memorial has always had special meaning for African Americans. This was especially true in 1939, when Marian Anderson, a black contralto, was barred from singing at D.C.'s Constitution Hall because of her race. Rather than give up, she simply changed the venue, and on Sunday, April 9, she performed a spellbinding concert on the steps of the Lincoln Memorial. 75,000 people gathered to hear her sing; millions more listened on the radio. A mural at the Interior Department commemorates the historic concert.

15

M is for Mall

The area south of Pennsylvania Avenue, between the Capitol and the Potomac River, is known as the National Mall. More than any other place in the country, it is where Americans gather to protest, to inspire, and to let their feelings be known. The Mall is America's soapbox. Here, in the shadow of the Washington Monument, is where democracy functions in its truest form.

Micromanage

George Washington, whose responsibility it was to get the federal city up and running, was a hands-on sort of supervisor—or, as we might say today, a micromanager. He involved himself in every aspect of the capital's construction. He hired and fired people. He pored over maps and blueprints. He determined the size of joints and rafters. He watched as wells were dug (and complained about their cost). He even decided how brightly polished Washington's curbstones should be! No detail was too small to escape his eye.

Money

The U.S. Bureau of Engraving and Printing is where America's paper money is printed. Tours are held daily. Unfortunately, there are no free samples.

Bags of real money are sold at discounted prices at the Bureau of Engraving and Printing. The catch? All the bills are shredded.

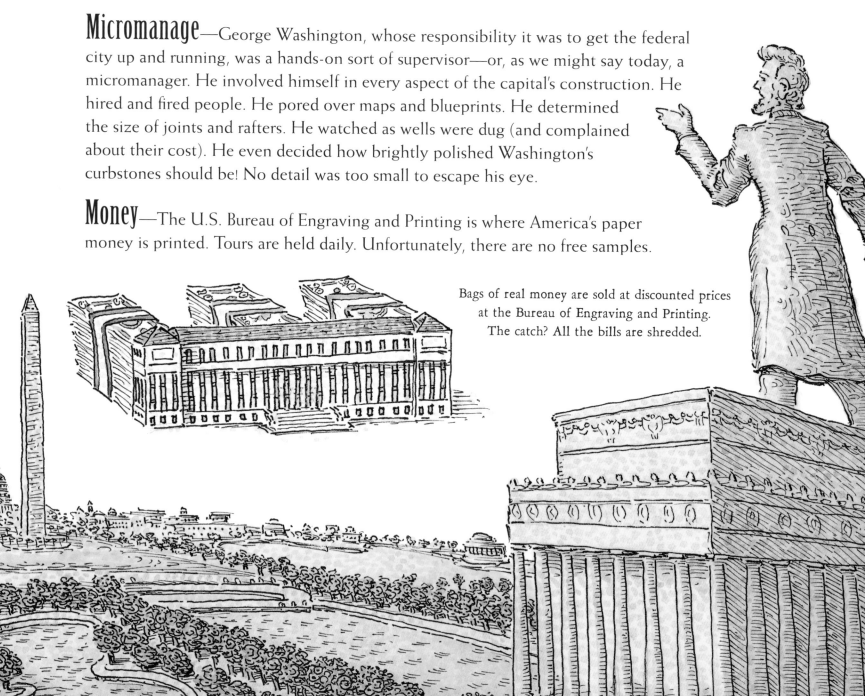

N is for National Archives

The National Archives in Washington is America's attic. Here are stored our most cherished documents, including the Declaration of Independence, the Constitution, the Bill of Rights, Washington's Farewell Address—even the check that we signed to buy Alaska from the Russians. The National Archives also has a large genealogy department, where people can trace their family trees.

In addition to documents, many unusual objects have been stored at the Archives. They include a mummified rat (a hit with school groups), a lady's glove with a map of London drawn on it, a pair of pajamas, a half-eaten hamburger, and an olive jar with two fingers in it. An entire book could be written about all the things to be found in "America's attic."

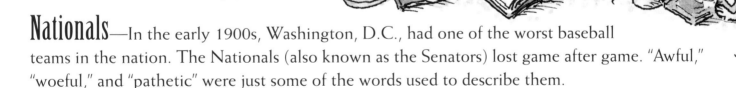

Nationals
—In the early 1900s, Washington, D.C., had one of the worst baseball teams in the nation. The Nationals (also known as the Senators) lost game after game. "Awful," "woeful," and "pathetic" were just some of the words used to describe them.

Nicknames
—Over the years, Washington has been given many nicknames. The nicer ones include the American Rome and the Capital of the World. Among the not-so-nice ones: Murder Capital of America and Hollywood for Ugly People.

"Most Americans have a very personal feeling about Washington and want to be proud of it."
ARCHITECT NATHANIEL A. OWINGS, 1968

17

O is for Obelisk

The Washington Monument is the tallest obelisk in the world. Because obelisks are Egyptian in origin, someone suggested to the government that the monument be accompanied by an enormous sphinx, one with an American eagle's head. That idea, fortunately, went nowhere.

Office Seeker—Washington, D.C., has always been full of office seekers—men and women seeking some kind of government position, preferably one that pays well and doesn't require much work. Ridding the White House of office seekers, Abraham Lincoln complained, was like "trying to shovel a bushel of fleas across a barn floor."

Organ—The Great Organ in Washington's National Cathedral is one of the largest in the world. It has more than 10,000 pipes!

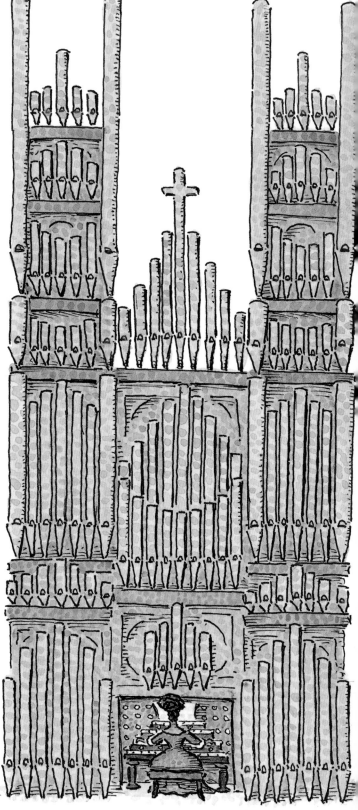

"What Washington needs is adult supervision."
SENATOR BARACK OBAMA, 2006

-18-

P is for Pennsylvania Avenue

As the main artery that connects the Capitol and the White House, Pennsylvania Avenue is Washington's most important street. It is on this wide thoroughfare that Washingtonians gather to watch inaugural parades; to celebrate military or political victories; to welcome home returning soldiers; or to honor a national hero, like astronaut John Glenn, who orbited Earth in 1962.

An especially large parade took place on Pennsylvania Avenue in 1913, when 8,000 women from all over the country marched, demanding their right to vote. Men snickered, but the laugh was on them. In 1920, women in America won the right to vote.

Potomac

Potomac—One reason George Washington located the nation's capital on the Potomac was because he believed that the river would become a great waterway, or highway, to the West. While that never happened, the Potomac is still vitally important to Washington: it provides 90 percent of the capital's drinking water.

Post

Post—Washington, D.C., may be the only city in America that has had a piece of music written to honor its local newspaper. In 1889, bandleader and composer John Philip Sousa wrote a lively march called "The Washington Post," which became one of his most popular compositions.

Musician Duke Ellington was born in Washington, D.C.

Q is for Quaker

Philadelphia was the nation's temporary capital from 1790 to 1800. It might well have remained the capital had it not been for the city's large Quaker population and their fierce opposition to slavery. Southern politicians would not allow the U.S. capital to be in a city—any city—that promoted emancipation. As one Southerner put it, he would rather pitch his tent beneath "a hornet's nest" than "vote for placing the government in a settlement of Quakers."

Quadruple—Between 1860 and 1870, Washington's black population almost quadrupled—from 14,000 to almost 44,000. Most of the newcomers were uneducated field hands from the South. Such a radical change in the makeup of society upset white Washingtonians, and for decades thereafter, discrimination was an ugly fact of life in the nation's capital.

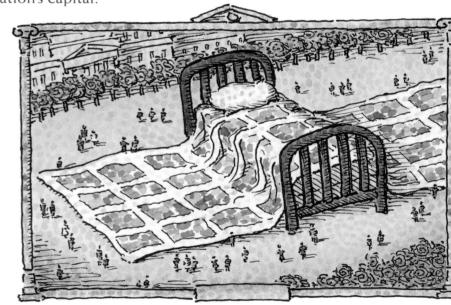

Quilt—The AIDS Memorial Quilt was first displayed to the public in 1987 in Washington, D.C. Made up of decorated panels of fabric stitched together, the colorful quilt contained the names of more than 8,000 people and was larger than a football field.

"I stand by all the misstatements that I've made."
VICE PRESIDENT DAN QUAYLE, 1989

R is for Rotunda

When presidents, politicians, and eminent citizens die, their bodies often lie in state in the Rotunda of the U.S. Capitol. When President John F. Kennedy was assassinated in 1963, a quarter of a million people filed slowly through the Rotunda to view his flag-draped casket. Civil rights activist Rosa Parks, who died in 2005, is the only woman whose body has lain in state in the Rotunda.

Rock Creek Cemetery

—Dedicated in 1719, Rock Creek Cemetery is the oldest cemetery in Washington, D.C. Upton Sinclair, a famous muckraking American writer, is buried here. So is Alice Roosevelt Longworth, Teddy Roosevelt's outspoken daughter. She's the one who said, "If you haven't got anything nice to say about anybody, come sit next to me."

Road

—In Washington's early days, the streets and roads were in such dreadful condition that carriages often overturned. "The roads are never repaired," one visitor complained. "Deep ruts, rocks, and stumps of trees, every minute impede your progress, and often threaten your limbs with dislocation."

"Politics is not a bad profession. If you succeed there are many rewards, if you disgrace yourself you can always write a book." PRESIDENT RONALD REAGAN

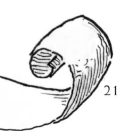

21

S is for Smithsonian

In 1829, an Englishman named James Smithson left half a million dollars to the city of Washington. According to his will, the money was to be used "for the increase . . . of knowledge among men." Amazingly, Congress nearly refused the gift. As one senator said, "It is beneath our dignity to accept presents from anyone."

Fortunately, wiser heads prevailed, but even then there was little agreement about how the money should be spent. Should it be used to build a school? A museum? A national university? These were questions not easily answered. In the end, the money was used to build the Smithsonian, one of the largest museums and research centers in the world. James Smithson would be pleased.

"America has the best politicians money can buy."
HUMORIST WILL ROGERS

"It is easier to do a job right than to explain why you didn't."
PRESIDENT MARTIN VAN BUREN

Slave—Many hundreds of slaves helped to build Washington, D.C. The U.S. government hired them from their owners for about fifteen cents a day. The slaves fired bricks, laid foundations, erected walls, felled trees, mixed mortar, quarried stone, and, with the help of horses and cattle, removed stumps to clear the way for future roads and streets.

Smelly—In its early days, when sanitation was poor, Washington was a smelly place. As one newspaperman put it: "It [is] impossible to move in any direction without keeping a hand to the nose."

Star-Spangled Banner—Because it survived a desperate battle fought during the War of 1812, the Star-Spangled Banner is America's most famous flag. It once flew over Fort McHenry, in Maryland, but today it can be found in Washington, at the National Museum of American History. The enormous flag, measuring thirty by forty-two feet, cost a little over $400 to make in 1813. Its value today? Priceless.

Street—In 1908, Gabby Street, a local ballplayer, caught a baseball that was dropped from the top of the Washington Monument. The ball was going 125 miles per hour when it slammed into Street's mitt. People said the moment of impact sounded like a pistol shot.

T is for Tractorcade

In February of 1979, 6,000 farmers came to Washington to protest the government's farm policy. They did not arrive in cars, in buses, or on the train. They rode their tractors to Washington! Soon the streets around the Capitol were filled with thousands of earthmovers, grass cutters, tillers, sweepers, loaders, and threshers. The big, noisy event was dubbed Tractorcade.

Telegraph—The world's first telegraphic message was sent from Washington, D.C., to Baltimore, Maryland, in 1844. The four-word message—a series of dots and dashes—read: "What hath God wrought?" What, indeed! A new era of long-distance communication had arrived.

Thunderstorm—On the night when the British burned the Capitol and the White House—August 24, 1814—a thunderstorm broke out in Washington. The heavy rain was the only thing that saved the entire city from going up in flames.

Tunnel—Underground tunnels connect all of the buildings in the U.S. Capitol Complex. An efficient electric tramway system whisks people from one location to the next.

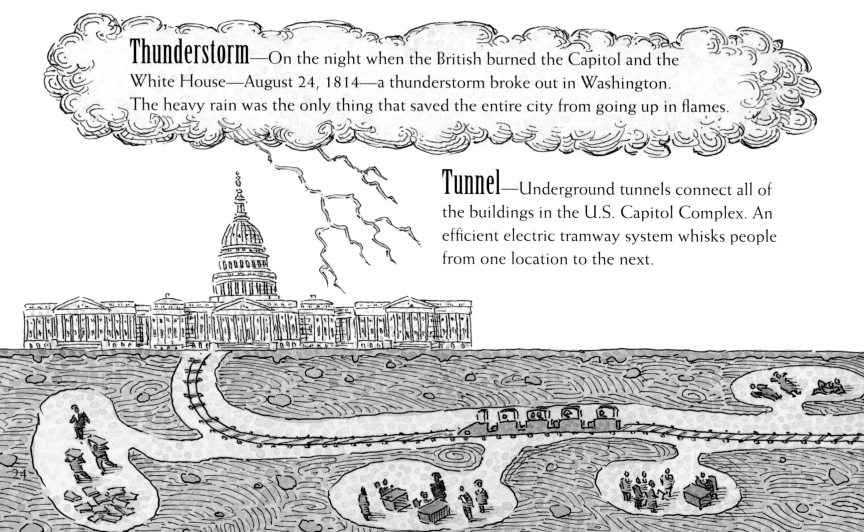

Tiger—In 1813, a 400-pound tiger and an African ape were exhibited in front of the Capitol. Washingtonians, who did not yet have a zoo, flocked to see the wild animals. The crowds were especially large each night at seven thirty, when the tiger was fed ten pounds of meat.

Telephone—Telephones were something new in the 1870s. Only a few could be found in Washington, D.C., but the White House had one. Its telephone number was easy to remember: 1. The number has since been changed.

25

U is for Unhealthy

Washington opened for business in 1800. Soon after, people began to complain that the city was a very unhealthy place. Year after year, the capital suffered outbreaks of typhoid, dysentery, cholera, malaria, and fever. Some blamed the humidity, others the mosquitoes, still others the garbage- and sewage-filled canal that ran through the heart of the city. Not until after World War I did sanitation methods improve.

Unpaved—Because it was unpaved for many years, Pennsylvania Avenue was a messy street to cross. In hot weather, your boots were covered with dust; in wet weather, with mud. But there was relief: on the opposite curb stood boys with buckets, sponges, and brushes, ready to clean your dirty shoes for a few pennies.

Unescorted—Until 1881, when James Garfield was assassinated, presidents often rode or walked about Washington unescorted. You never knew where they might turn up.

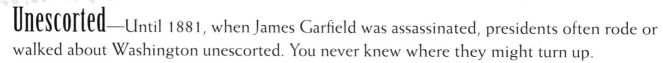

Some scientists believe that, because of climate change, Washington could be underwater by the year 2100.

V is for Vietnam Veterans

Ever since it opened in 1982, the Vietnam Veterans Memorial has been one of Washington's most sought-out destinations. Here, on two long black walls, are listed the names of those Americans who lost their lives in the Vietnam War, which lasted from 1955 to 1975. The soldiers' names are listed not alphabetically, but in the order in which they died. Also listed are the names of those who went missing in action. Every day, people can be seen at the site, taking rubbings of the names of their loved ones. Though it represents great grief, the Vietnam Veterans Memorial provides most Americans with a much-needed feeling of peace, and of closure. The wall wounds, but it also heals.

Vacant—Thomas Jefferson, our third president, always left Washington during the summer months to escape the heat and humidity. Other people followed his example, leaving their homes vacant and unwatched. Burglars were thrilled. They were happy to work in the heat.

WHITE HOUSE

132 ROOMS

28 FIREPLACES

VACANCY

W is for White House

The White House was the first federal building erected in Washington, D.C. John Adams, who spent only a few months there, didn't care for it. Neither did his wife, Abigail. She found it too cold. Thomas Jefferson thought it was too big for the head of a republic, calling it "a great stone house, big enough for two emperors, one pope and the grand lama into the bargain." (But that didn't stop him from moving in.) Nearly every president since Jefferson has complained about the White House's lack of privacy. Nevertheless, it is America's most famous home, and despite its inconveniences, most politicians would love to live there.

MOVERS

The tip of the Washington Monument is made of aluminum, a rare and costly metal in the 1880s when the monument was completed.

Washington Monument—Over five hundred feet tall, the Washington Monument is a striking piece of architecture. Upon its completion in 1884, it was the tallest structure in the world. It took many years to build and underwent many changes along the way. The original site chosen for it, in alignment with the Capitol and the White House, turned out to be too soggy to support such great weight. Had the monument been built there, it would have sunk in no time at all!

Weather Bureau—The Weather Bureau was established in Washington, D.C., in 1870. It was the nation's first attempt to track weather in all parts of the United States. Today the Weather Bureau is known as the National Weather Service.

Wildlife—In its early years, Washington, D.C., teemed with wildlife. Toads, turtles, rabbits, squirrels, ducks, snipe, and geese all made their home along the banks of the Potomac. The river itself was so full of fish, said one explorer, that they lay "with their heads out of the water."

HELLO MY NAME IS FEDERAL CITY

George Washington never called the U.S. capital "Washington." He was too modest for that. He always referred to it as "Federal City."

X is for Mei Xiang

One of Washington's most popular residents isn't a person, but an animal. Born in China in 1998, Mei Xiang is a female giant panda who lives at the National Zoo. "Giant" is right—she weighs over 230 pounds. Mei Xiang means "beautiful fragrance," and every day thousands of people log onto the zoo's "Panda Cam" to see what she and her cubs are up to.

X-1 and X-15—Two popular attractions at Washington's Air and Space Museum are the X-1 and the X-15. The X-1, built in 1945, was the rocket plane that broke the sound barrier in 1947. Pilot Chuck Yeager was at the controls. Also on display at Air and Space is an X-15, the fastest plane ever built. Powered by rockets, the X-15 can travel at an unbelievable 4,500 miles per hour!

Y is for Yellow Fever

In 1793, a devastating epidemic of yellow fever broke out in Philadelphia, then the nation's capital. Borne by mosquitoes, it killed thousands. People were so badly frightened by the epidemic that all talk ceased of making Philadelphia the permanent capital. As unlikely as it may sound, mosquitoes are part of the reason the U.S. capital is on the Potomac and not the Schuylkill River.

YMCA—Years ago, black Washingtonians were not welcome at the local YMCA, so they started their own. The "colored YMCA," as it was known, was especially popular with Washington's black ministers, who used the swimming pool for baptisms.

Z is for Zoo

The National Zoo is one of Washington's great attractions. Founded in 1889, the 163-acre zoo is home to more than 2,000 animals from 400 species. By far, the zoo's most famous resident was Smokey Bear, who lived there for twenty-six years. Smokey received so much fan mail that in 1964 the U.S. Postal Service gave him his own zip code!

Zorapteran—Entomology, the study of insects, is a big part of the Smithsonian's National Museum of Natural History. Here visitors can view 35 million specimens, everything from aphids to zorapterans.

And back to A . . .

A is for America

Washington, D.C., is more than simply a capital city. It is, and always has been, a symbol of America itself. The Capitol, the Washington Monument, the Lincoln Memorial, protests at the Mall, celebrations on Pennsylvania Avenue—these things are fundamentally American. They are part of who we are as a people.

Some cities seem frozen in time. But not Washington. Our capital is always changing, attempting to become something stronger and more truly democratic. In that respect, Washington is not just a city in America. It is America.

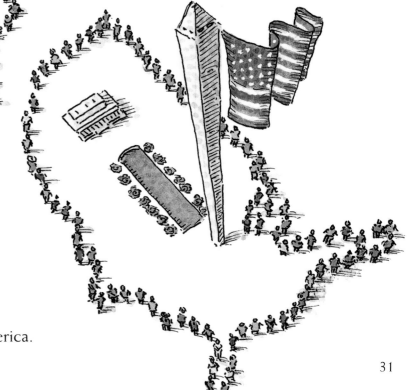

"To the City of Washington: the central star of
the constellation which enlightens the world."
A toast given in 1824 by
the Marquis de Lafayette,
French patriot of the American Revolution

For source notes see www.holidayhouse.com
The map of the District of Columbia on the endpapers was created by
cartographer Tom Patterson for the U.S. National Park Service.

Text copyright © 2018 by Alan Schroeder
Illustrations copyright © 2018 by John O'Brien
All Rights Reserved
HOLIDAY HOUSE is registered in the U.S. Patent and Trademark Office
Printed and bound in November 2017 at Toppan Leefung, DongGuan City, China.
www.holidayhouse.com
First Edition
1 3 5 7 9 10 8 6 4 2

Library of Congress Cataloging-in-Publication Data
Names: Schroeder, Alan, author. | O'Brien, John, 1953–illustrator.
Title: Washington, D.C.: our nation's capital from A–Z / by Alan Schroeder;
illustrated by John O'Brien.
Description: New York: Holiday House, 2018.
Identifiers: LCCN 2017006714 | ISBN 9780823436781 (hardcover)
Subjects: LCSH: Washington (D.C.)—Juvenile literature.
Classification: LCC F194.3.S37 2018 | DDC 975.3—dc23 LC record available at https://lccn.loc.gov/2017006714

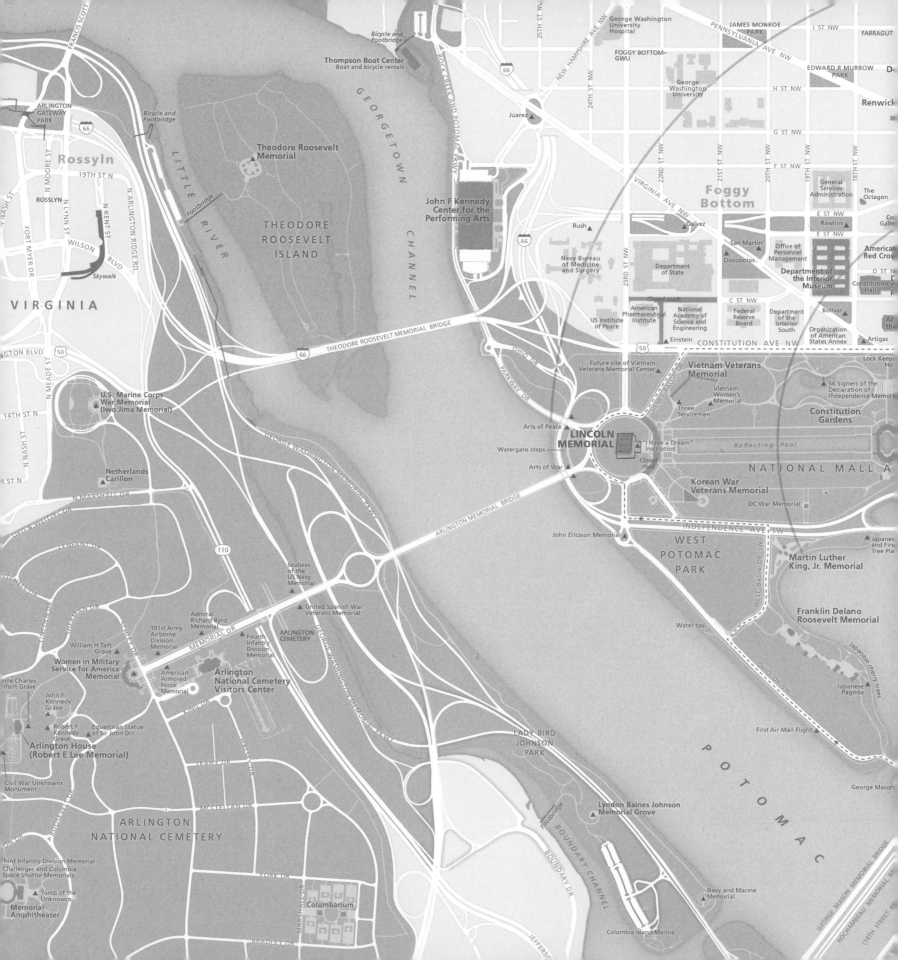